HOOE and TURNCHAPEL REMEMBERED

Arthur L. Clamp

The attractive scene of Hooe Lake shows Cecil Doney in his boat
making for the old Shute Quay. The lake was filled in 1964.

This version of the book is virtually as originally published.
There are now additional pages at the back providing information about the author.

The republishing project is being managed by Arthur's grandson, Steven Gibson. We aim to find all the research that he was involved in publishing, preserving it for the next generation as part of 'The Clamp Collection'.

INTRODUCTION

THIS illustrated booklet looks back over the past eighty years and recalls scenes, people and events which went towards making up part of the Hooe and Turnchapel communities. Many other aspects of the area will go unrecorded and will probably fade from the memory but in putting together this title it is hoped that something of the days gone past will find a place among someone's library or bookshelf and be of pleasure to the coming generations. The book should not be taken as a precise record of these years but, perhaps more as a patchwork view remembered by many local folk and recorded through photographs they took with box or similar cameras.

Hooe and Turnchapel now make up part of a very large area of development on the south side of the Cattewater which takes in Oreston, Pomphlett, Plymstock, Billacombe, Elburton, Goosewell and Staddiscombe. The dramatic changes of recent years have affected local patterns of living and work and changed the landscape and views of many once well known localities including those in this book. The roots of all these places go back many years and they can rightly claim to a past that is of equal interest to any in the land. In fact the communities bordering the Cattewater were additionally coloured by their maritime links and make subjects in themselves of special note.

Hooe like the Hoe in Plymouth takes its name from a "high place" and Turnchapel is thought to have been derived from St. Anne's Chapel to Tan Chapel and then to the present word. This stood at the head of Hooe Lake where services were held from about 1100 to at least the 1500s. Turnchapel itself had a Wesleyan Chapel which opened in 1816 with Henry Dean as "manager". This closed a few years ago and the building was then converted into a private dwelling. St. John's Church, Hooe, was consecrated on 25th September, 1855, by the Bishop of Exeter, then the parish of Hooe was created two years later in 1857. This is now the main place of worship for the two communities.

Although records of some activity at Turnchapel go back to the 1200s it did not come into its own until the early 1800s when a dry dock was built where Isaac Blackburn built two ships, the *Armada* and the *Clarence*. Both carried 74 guns and were the largest ships then built outside of the Dockyard. Ship building of one form or another has continued at Turnchapel although the style of boats have changed over the years. Wooden sailing craft, fishing boats and Tamar barges could once be seen on the stocks; now it is the turn of pleasure craft and these occupy slipways and give employment in the locality. There were a number of small shipyards along the Cattewater from Mount Batten up to Oreston and down the opposite bank.

Ferry boats under Mr. H. R. Elford's Oreston and Turnchapel Steam Boat Company linked the area with Plymouth which did champion service with the red funnelled steamers. Fourteen boats have seen service in this company between 1862 and 1957. The old steam railway and then buses picked up the passenger trade into the city especially after the tolls were abolished on Laira Bridge in 1924. The railway served both Oreston and Turnchapel from the late 1890s to the line closure to passenger traffic in 1951.

Industry and trade have left their marks on the areas mainly in form of disused quarries once worked for the still plentiful limestone where some of it was burnt in nearby limekilns for agricultural use. A lot of stone left the area for building and road making. Hexton Hill Quarry being one of the most interesting remains from this activity. A full catalogue of trades for both places would be surprisingly long. Fishermen, pilots, shipwrights, rope makers, boat builders, carpenters, cordwainers, then lime burners, quarrymen, farmers, labourers, herdsmen, shop keepers, grocers, coal merchants, bakers, landlords of the various inns and many others have worked in one way or another here close to the banks of the Plym.

Change has come about here as elsewhere more so after the last war in which both places suffered damage and casualties. The blazing oil tanks at Turnchapel are still well remembered by many people when they lit up the night sky and burnt uncontrolled for some days. The ferry link over the entrance to Hooe Lake has gone, the swing bridge taken up, Hooe Lake filled in, some roads widened, a new use for Fort Stamford has been found, shops are giving wider service to people, the infant school opened in 1956 and a host of other changes are shaping Hooe and Turnchapel at a rate never seen before.

I am most grateful to many people for their help in advising me on the preparation of this book but I must select Mr. and Mrs. H. Hurrell and Arthur and Doreen Glinn for expressing my direct thanks for without their help this book would not have been possible in this form. Finally may this title be a reminder of many features of these two very interesting localities.

Arthur L. Clamp,
December, 1981.

Three Views of the Area

This view shows Hooe School in the middle distance then Hooe Lake backed by part of Turnchapel. The two local farmers, Mr. Sherrell and Mr. Harris grazed cattle on the fields in the foreground which are now built upon. The manually operated railway swing bridge joins Oreston to Turnchapel.

Hooe Lake

Part of the lake at high water enabled local boat owners to come right up to the main road in small craft as seen here with two boats in view. The road, however, to Hexton Hill was flooded on occasions close to where the two parked cars are in front of the *Royal Oak*. The lake was filled in in recent years (1964) and now forms a green on which some village activities take place. Shute Quay was to the left of the picture.

Looking towards Higher Hooe

This is almost the opposite view to the upper one taken from where the oil tanks are hidden by earth and grass and occupying part of an old quarry. This is on the high ground set back from Turnchapel. The fields and openness of Hooe is very evident in this scene showing to good effect the woods crowning the higher land.

Farming at Hooe

This is one of the very few photographs taken of a local farming scene once such an important part of this area. Mr. Southern is here raking over hay where St. John's, Hooe, football pitch now is set against the background of the wooded hillside and Hooe Manor on the far left side of the scene.

Harris's Tree and Fruit Garden

Mrs. Kate Harris is here at the front of the once very popular tea gardens venue of many a group of adults and Sunday School scholars out from Plymouth for the day. She and her husband kept cows and ran a milk round. Frank Harriss took over the gardens which were listed as far back as 1890 then run by Thomas Harris. The *Mount Batten Inn* now stands on the site of this building latterly occupied by Mr. Savery.

The new Community Centre

A recent event of great local importance was the opening of the Hooe and Turnchapel Community Centre on the 25th April, 1981, by Deputy Lord Mayor, Councillor Gordon Draper. Here he is unveilling the wall plaque and notice watched by Mrs. Susan Tribble, Derek England, Roy Wallace, the local community constable standing next to the Chief Constable John Anderson.

Down at Sycamore Beach

This picture, probably dating from around 1930, shows one of the many and very popular Turnchapel carnival events held at "Sycamore" a spot at the waterside named after the tree in the photograph. This is no longer standing but memories of the annual swimming, diving and other water sports are still strong in the minds of many local people. Here can be seen a waterman's boat, *The Two Sisters*, with Tisher Dungey and Tedman Elliott and behind them Sadder Oxland in another boat. These sports closed around the start of the last war.

Hooe Manor

This is one of the imposing buildings in the locality originally called Belleview but later changed by the Bulteel family to the existing name although it has never been a manor house in the normally accepted sense. The Georgian building dates from 1777 and during the period shown here was occupied by Colonel and Mrs. Coates who were great supporters at St. John's Church and other local groups.

An Annual Outing

An event of more recent years was this outing, one of many for the area, organised by Mr. Mitcheson. They are about to set off for the day and include Fred Thomas, Jim Demellweek, John Gray, Len Roberts, Arthur Glinn, Billy Perry, Eric Gray, Harry Skilton, Bobby Burridge, Malley Burridge, Douglas Mutton, Albert Pearse, Tom Lawrence and many other local men.

The Castle Inn, Mount Batten

This delightful picture of the inn which formerly stood close to the old tower or castle was taken in 1887. The building was demolished in 1962 to make way for the present Sergeants' mess on the R.A.F. Station, although it had lost its licence to sell beer and liquor many years before. The inn served the thousands of Plymothians who used to go over to the spot by ferry boat from the Barbican on holidays and it was also a frequent haunt of people living on this side of the Plym as well. George Hine, J. H. Watts and F. T. Webb were the landlords at various times. There were also tea gardens close by.

The *Lively* Ferry

This was one of the many local popular ferry boats which worked between Oreston, Turnchapel and Plymouth. This shows her there sometime before 1914 as during the Great War she was chartered as a liberty boat. She later returned to the company and was sold in 1951.

Looking towards Radford
The circular mound of earth in the foreground clearly shows the shape of an underlying oil tank used for storage and now hidden to sight. The old Turnchapel railway line is to the left while to the right of the lake are some moored house-boats occupying parts of the foreshore. Radford Castle can be identified behind which Plymstock starts.

Crowning the Carnival Queen in 1949
Part of the local carnival is the very important ceremony of crowning a queen. Here can be seen the then local vicar, Rev. L. E. H. Pike placing the crown on the head of Vera Becker, with Jean Carpenter and Sylvia Hurrell in attendance at Turnchapel Methodist church.

Hooe and Turnchapel Carnival
The spirit of a post-war carnival is reflected in the smiles, manner and dress of Phyllis Pascoe and Dorothy Wells as they sell small items to visitors dressed as maidens.

Two Local Football Teams

The upper group comprises of Boringdon A.F.C. in the middle 1930s seen here on their home pitch at Hexton Wood. The team members are J. Oates, F. Boobier, A. Glinn, R. Lillicrap, R. Tucker, T. Benmore, H. Gilpin, A. Pearse, B. Skilton, J. Twichen, D. Skilton, W. Gale, H. Doddridge, W. Roberts, J. Pearson, W. Salmon, T. Lillicrap and A. Thomas. The lower team is for the season 1906-7, Turnchapel A.F.C., with Rev. F. Gilbertson, Dort Pascho, S. Hocking, J. Simmons, W. Alsop, W. Williams, W. Kellaway, H. Copp, J. Rowse, W. North, captain, W. Venus, C. Fielder, S. Tozer, and S. Shillabeer. They held the cup for the first division of the Devon League.

Extracts from Henry J. Hurrell's Diary

19th January, 1928: "Palace Saloon" buses commenced from Hooe to Plymouth. Mr. Harold Dolton the first passenger. Taken over by Western National Bus Co. later.

3rd March, 1928: "Eddystone" Bus Service commenced at Hooe.

5th March, 1928: Gas lamps erected at Turnchapel in street.

4th July, 1928: First Hooe Church Fete held in Harris's Tea Gardens. Rev. Turquand.

14th August, 1928 Porpoise in Hooe Lake.

16th November, 1928: S.S. *Kentish Coast* wrecked on Batten Beach.

21st November, 1928: Diphtheria bad in this district.

4th February, 1929: Magic Lantern Lecture at Hooe Church for "Waifs and Strays".

3rd March, 1929: Hooe Schools (Sunday and Day) closed owing to diphtheria.

5th October, 1929: Severe gale here - several trees blown down - 1 big tree at Radford.

5th December, 1929: Severe gale until 8th - gale force reaches 107 m.p.h.

27th January, 1930: Airship R.100 flew over Hooe - trial trip.

5th July, 1930: G.W.R. closes Yealmpton line for passenger traffic (re-opened again on 3rd November, 1941).

27th October, 1930: Building of new school at Hooe commenced.

3rd May, 1931: Hooe St. Johns Football Club received Senior Cup at Co-operative House Frank Boobier captain.

5th October, 1931: New School at Hooe commences. Turnchapel Juniors and Higher School unite. Officially opened on 12th October by Sir Francis Ackland.

6th November, 1931: Roads lit by electricity from Radford to top of Hooe.

January, 1932: Bungalow next to Hooe House (Glinns) completed and occupied.

1st March, 1932: Council houses at Hooe being occupied (first time).

13th April, 1932: Staddiscombe policeman approached four motor bandits in a stolen car at Bovisand Lane and was forced to abandon the car at point of three revolvers. Car stolen at Chudleigh and abandoned at Mount Gold.

13th April, 1932: Electric light cable laid outside our house (Croft Cottage).

14th May, 1932: Mr. E. Wakeham (Butcher) closes business, ill health.

10th July, 1932: Bishop of Exeter visited Hooe Church 3 p.m. Choir and Parochial Church Council and church wardens met him at gate and led him into the Church singing hymn 211 A. & M.

15th August, 1932: Hooe streets lit up by electricity for the first time.

22nd August, 1932: Our house wired for electric light (Croft Cottage).

4th January, 1933: Road widening commenced from Hooe corner opposite school to Bottom of Belle View Hill by F.J. Moore (Quarry) and earth from Banks, etc. etc. tipped in old Quarry (Hexton).

18th January, 1933: Last of big trees cut down at Harris's corner by Mr. Mitchell.

13th February, 1933: Mr. Tapper's shop opened at Chute Quay (Lake Stores).

13th February, 1933: Mr. Stansbury (Schoolmaster) comes to Hooe.

28th June, 1933: Mrs. Perry's shop (Post Office) completed and opened (Lake Road).

18th February, 1934: A swan breaks its leg on the foreshore of Hooe Lake, near Chute Quarry Mrs. Coates phones to the R.S.P.C.A. and they take it away by motor.

22nd January, 1935: Five men gassed while digging a trench at Hooe at the bottom of Church Hill and puncturing a gas main. All the five men were employees of the Plymouth Gas Company and they all recovered by artificial respiration.

1st March, 1935: Two seamen fight on Timber boat, one stabs the other and kills him.

23rd June, 1935: Last tree up Church Hill by Cliff Gate cut down (left side) all cut down in about two weeks.

8th July, 1935: During the week building of houses commenced on the left of Church Hill.

July, 1935: Hedge of road from the top of Radford Hill to Repath's corner torn down and road widening in operation (left side).

10th February, 1936: Strong easterly gale and a coal barge swept by a huge wave and overturns in Plymouth Sound. Two Millbrook men drowned.

20th April, 1936: Mr. Rowe started to clear trees, etc. from site at Harris's Tea Gardens, to build Hooe Social Club.

25th August, 1936: Hooe held its first Carnival at Hexton Path Field.

Summer, 1936: During the Summer Radford House (Mansion) demolished by Triggs Contractor for the purpose of building houses on the estate. Later the contractor went bankrupt and no houses were built.

24th November, 1936: Rev. Bridger inducted at Hooe Church.

31st December, 1936: Hooe Social Club opened at 6.30 p.m. for members to form a committee. Bar and Billiards open to members.

4th March, 1937: Talkie films at Hooe Social Club—first ever shown in Hooe

5th April, 1937: Election of Rural District Council held at Hooe School.

17th June, 1937: Belisha Beacon erected at Hooe opposite school.

21st February, 1938: During this week lime kiln re-opened and used at Moore's Quarry. Rubble banks after 52 years idle.

October, 1938: Work commenced at Radford to build oil tanks underground for the Mount Batten Air Force. Wimpey's of London contractors employing Irishmen.

23rd February, 1939: Motor excavator commenced to dig next to Sherrill's farm for a pumping station. One building already commenced about two weeks ago.

April, 1939: Wimpey's of London commenced to remove the rubble bank by Turnchapel Station to make room for sidings. The rubble used to bury oil tanks at Radford.

June, 1939: W. Larcombe the first man at Hooe to be examined for the Militia (This being the first year).

8th January, 1940: Sylvia starts school at Hooe. Mr. Rabley, headmaster. Miss Lovell class teacher.

17th January, 1940: Hooe Lake frozen across from southern end down to opposite Royal Oak.

21st January, 1940: Bishop of Plymouth (Rev. Daukes) visited Hooe Church and attended 11 a.m. service officiated by Rev. Bridger after visiting troops.

January, 1940: Early this month work on pipe line from Turnchapel Wharf to Radford completed and tested.

2nd June, 1940: French and other troops arrive at Turnchapel station (600) from Dunkirk.

June, 1940: Railings being fixed round Shute Quay from around the beach to Hooe Club and Post Office.

29th June, 1940: Saturday morning 12.45 approximately air raid alarm sounded here and Plymouth. All clear at 1.50 a.m. First raid: one plane (no firing) searchlight active.

8th July, 1940: Started to erect barricades, concrete blocks: squares filled with concrete and barbed wire on top outside our house.

24th August, 1940: Fire at Hooe Lake, petrol leaking from oil pipes. Special constables patrolling area stopping all cars and pedestrians and cautioning them against smoking. Pool petrol men salvaging petrol.

26th August, 1940: 13 high explosive bombs and 15 incendiaries dropped in Hooe. Damage done to two of Mr. Rowe's flats and craters in fields from Stadden to Hexton Hill.

5th October, 1940: Air raid shelters erection commenced at Hooe.

27th November, 1940: One alert at 3.50 p.m. and one raid from 6.30 p.m. till 2.30 a.m. W. Burgoynes house and Nos. 5 and 6 of Rowe's flats down. Bomb craters in Mr. Harris's orchard, Harwoods and two at Mr. Ball's. Oil tanks at Turnchapel on fire lasting till Sunday. Damage done to Mount Batten. Two people, Mr. and Mrs. Farrow, killed in Mr. Rowe's flats, Mrs. Burgoyne, Betty and Derrick and Mrs. Charles and four children killed downstairs, making a total of 10 dead.

28th November, 1940: Bombs dropped at Prince Rock, also Jennycliffe Gate, also Hooe Church Yard. Voluntary evacuation of children and adults from Hooe to Plymstock and Goosewell Schools at night owing to danger from blazing oil tanks—one explodes during the night and Hooe Lake catches fire, and two during day. All village evacuated to Plympton at night until Sunday night.

8th December, 1940: Strong gangs of men working at Turnchapel Station relaying lines and timbers in Station and first part of Bridge, damage caused by fire from oil tanks on November 27th - no trains since.

16th December, 1940: Trains started to run off Turnchapel branch line.

20th October, 1943: Balloon gets out of control in field behind school and comes down in Mr. Ford's farm and explodes and catches farm house on fire.

January, 1944: Road widening commenced from bottom of Belle View Hill to Radford by private contract.

28th April, 1944: Sun. 1st April raid—damage at Oreston—15 cows killed at Radford (Mr. Phillips)—several people killed at Oreston.

1st September, 1945: Hooe Victory V.J. Carnival held in schoolroom (wet weather).

April, 1946: Wall being built down Radford Hill on right—old wall torn down to widen road in January 1944.

4th October, 1946: Rev. A. Fry inducted to Hooe Church by Bishop of Plymouth and Rural Dean Rev. Bennett.

17th March, 1947: During this week air raid shelters in Hooe demolished at Yonder Street and school shelters dug up at Penny Park.

November, 1947: Second lot (18 Council houses) being built at the rear of Meadow View first two let in July

February, 1948: Hooe Manor, late Col. Coates residence and estate and previous to this date bought by Devon County Council for £9,000 as a home for aged people, which was turned down and converted into flats at 35/- per week. Five flats made and three let to employees of the Council. Strong protests made by Parish Council regarding the system of secretly allocating these flats and in future the allocation to be incorporated with the Council Housing scheme and advertised.

28th September, 1948: Rev. Pike inducted to Hooe Church by the Bishop of Plymouth.

8th August, 1949: Workmen commenced alterations to Harris's Barn and shippen to make a fish and chip shop. Front of building torn down and rebuilt. Mr. Savery having work done. (Shop opened 5th January, 1950).

21st August, 1949: New bus service commenced from St. Andrew's Cross to Mount Batten.
17th April, 1950: Commenced to dig wall to build public lavatories at Hooe.
November, 1950: Public lavatories opposite Hooe Social Club opened for use.
8th September, 1951: Turnchapel branch of British Railways closed to passenger transport. Last train left Turnchapel for Friary at 10.45 p.m. (service commenced 4th October, 1896).
16th March, 1952: Electric light used for the first time at Hooe St. Johns Church.
1st October, 1953: Seat placed by Council under school wall.
December, 1954: Four flats let at Lilac Close, first of new Council houses.
6th June, 1955: Work commenced this week on new School site opposite Victoria Inn.
25th September, 1955: Centenary Service held at Hooe Church—Bishop of Exeter preached sermon at Evensong.
February, 1956: All Council houses on new estate comprising South Hill, etc., completed.
September, 1956: A new school (Hooe Infants) costing £25,582 opened to relieve congestion at Hooe Junior School.
29th October, 1956: Hooe Infants School officially opened by Lady Roborough. Parts of school used from September.
April, 1957: New houses in Mr. Savery's Orchard—first lot built and occupied. Named *The Green*.
29th May, 1957: Mr. Hobbs opened Fish and Chip shop after being closed by Mr. Savery.
2nd August, 1957: New street lamps lit at Hooe.
9th November, 1958: War Memorial at Hooe Church unveiled by Mrs. K. Tucker.
24th September, 1959: Bus Shelter being erected at Hooe, Shute Quay.
August, 1960: First week. Foundations dug for roads, etc. for new estate in fields from Primary School to Brakes' bottom field.
10th March, 1961: Hooe Social Club struck off register for 12 months.
24th June, 1961: Hooe School Bathing Pool opened. Fete held in school grounds raising £350. Mr. R. Fice, headmaster.
August, 1961: Hooe School iron spiked railings replaced by wire mesh fencing.
12th November, 1961: Hooe Baptist Church holds first Baptismal Service, Susan Dent.
23rd November, 1961: Graddon & Sons opened new shop in Belle Vue Estate.
February, 1962: Road widening commenced at Radford bottom. River piped and trees cut down opposite farm. Underlane being widened on debris tip at bottom to fill in dip.
6th June, 1962: Sun fish weighing 180 lbs caught in Hooe Lake—taken to Plymouth Aquarium.
9th July, 1962: Hooe Social Club re-opens under new management.
6th May, 1963: Bulldozer started to knock down three cottages on top of Hexton Hill took three days and rubble and debris tipped into Hooe Lake round the beach.
August, 1963: New sewerage work commenced at Radford (Flood Field) for Plymstock and Hooe. Earth and rock from field being tipped in Hooe Lake, to fill in top end from *Royal Oak* to Shute Quay.
7th October, 1963: Turnchapel Railway Swing Bridge being broken up for scrap.
February, 1964: Contractors started to build wall across Hooe Lake and rubble and earth brought from Hay Quarry, Stag Lodge and debris from houses being pulled down in Hooe Village under slum clearance scheme also from Plymouth Harvest Home and Breakwater Quarry for Gas Works - also pipes being laid to carry water from old Shute Quay and road surface water to the Lake.
19th July, 1964: Mr. Fletcher of Hooe Social Club burnt out the inside of Mr. Savery's house (previously Harris's Farm) the house to be demolished for extending Hooe Social Club and to make a car park at the rear. The house demolished by two bulldozers on Monday Tuesday and Wednesday. The Fish and Chip Shop which used to be the cow shippen and barn demolished on Thursday 13th August.
November, 1965: Hooe Sewerage Scheme started. Pump house in operation to sewerage plant at Kill Park, Radford.
25th February, 1966: Hooe Social Club renamed *Mount Batten* opened.
15th November, 1966: Trees planted on the Green at Hooe Lake.
February, 1967: Ford's farm at Hooe fields taken over by Wimpey for House building.
27th February, 1967: Wimpey commenced on Hooe Barton Farm with bulldozer knocking down railings of field in Jennycliffe Road.
1st April, 1967: Plymouth takes over parish of Plympton/Plymstock and part of Brixton in boundary extension.
May, 1967: Started fixing railings and posts for fence on Hooe Green—eight seats put on Green.
24th August, 1967: First of Wimpey houses occupied (Pollard Close).
5th November, 1968: First Naval house occupied opposite St. Johns Road.

15th September, 1969: Sherrell's Farm (Mr. Ford) farmhouse and shippen demolished to make way for shops on Wimpey estate.
9th April, 1970: Explosion at 4.50 a.m. at the Continental Oil Depot, Turnchapel Quarries, when first tanker driver arrived for duty and switched on electric switch, owing to a big petrol leak in a one million gallon tank and area and pipeline saturated. Petroleum only discharged from ship to tank the day before and man badly burnt and fires started in several places. The road around the Beach closed and firemen and police cordoned off the area. The tanker ship was recalled to draw off the petrol from the tank. People north of Westways and Lake Road and Hexton Hill evacuated to Plymstock School. On Friday 10th, petrol found to be floating on Hooe Lake - a boom was placed from the Boom Defence to Oreston - police ordered no naked lights and fires in people's houses. Wednesday 15th. People living outside danger area but close asked to move away from 10 a.m. to 6 p.m. accommodation provided at Norley Hall. All clear given by Chief Fuel Officer on Sunday 19th at 6 p.m.
29th October, 1970: Stamford Fort—built 1865—opened as a night club.
July, 1973: Hooe Churchyard closed to new graves.
21st September, 1973: Hooe Naval Community Centre opened.
11th February, 1974: Highest tides for 300 years. A wave of water came up Hooe Lake and swamped over roads (19ft.) Fire Brigade called to pump out houses. Jennycliffe Beach tea hut severely damaged by waves and quay partly washed away.
18th February, 1975: First tree planted at Radford Arboretum, a "Californian Redwood" among largest and oldest living trees in the world.
29th March, 1977: Wall of Bernard Stévan's garden knocked down to widen the road between the *Royal Oak* and the garden wall to allow house building up the road to Hexton Hill. Started building on left side of hill early April.
8th November, 1979: Plymouth City Lotteries granted £10,000 to help buy the Hooe and Turnchapel Community Centre from the Ministry of Defence (Naval) also £15,000 to Plymstock Community Centre. Hooe and Turnchapel Community Centre costing £15,000. Mr. R. Wallace, Hooe Constable, organiser and chairman.
13th December, 1979: Naval houses (bungalows) "Stamford Close" Hooe sold by auction, bought by Wallsend Property Sales.
26th September, 1980: 125th Dedication Festival of the Consecration of Hooe St. Johns Church—exhibition of photographs of records, people and events relating to the Church and district in the past.
17th December, 1980: Fish and Chips and take away shop opened at West Hooe.

Hooe and Turnchapel children of a few years ago

Mrs. S. Stankley cheerfully endorses the children's smiles in this group of a few years ago. Recognised among the youngsters are Michael Dawson, Annette Sleeman, Christine Watson, Irene Burridge, Richard Powell, Jill Leatherhead, Marlene Pope, Katherine May, Jennifer Fry, Catherine Brown, Dorothy Marlow, Susan Bate, Jean Smith, Wendy Milner and David Tugwell. The photograph below dates from 1957 and shows Mr. Slater with Jimmy Hosgood, Jonathan Brown, Elton Baker, Neil Robinson, Michael Goss, Roy Short, David Dean, Pam Burch, Susan Jones, Martyn Gill, Alan Hole, Susan Haines, Jessica Brim and Lesley Ainger. No doubt many others will be identified and recall memories of school days.

Children move from Hooe School, 1981

These groups show children who have completed their schooling at Hooe and have moved on to Plymstock in 1981. Miss I. M. Simkiss, headmistress, and Mrs. J. Millward are the staff with Sarah Fryer, Joanne Marsden, David Tilley, Anita Riggs, Katie Pow, Jenny Lowles, Gary Chiswell, Rhonda Martin, Andrea Knight, Mandy Hunwicks, Jules Knight, Colin Leslie, Anthony Campbell, Shaun Chrome, Darren Hitchcox, Rachel Lilley, Debra Coan, Lee Haisman, Davis Steels, Darrel Beck, Ann Richardson, Lucy Munday, Kerry Bennett, Alison Small, Peter Jones and Shane Fowler. Below is the headmistress, Mrs. A. Harber with class 4H, and Mark Burtwell, Paul Simpson, Beverley Fosh, Paul Clark, Louise Pearse, Tina Harris, Suzanne Fulford, Carole Dawson, Denise Jones, Natalie Hover, Bonnie Searle, Joanne Libby, Gill Murden, Sara Bernard, Lorraine Blackney, Steven Burridge, Paul Scoble, Trudi Beard, Rachel Glynn, John Wills, Heather Scarr, Joanna McGinnes, Jacquie Bond, Andrea Libby, Sean Farrell, Daniel Watson, Richard Paterson, Christopher Howe, Stephen Hocking and Jason Rawlings.

Ladies at the Wellfield

The Wellfield at Turnchapel acted in many respects as a village green where all sorts of events used to take place. Here a group of local ladies pose for the photographer probably sometime in the late 1920s. Mrs. O. Roberts, Mrs. E. Wells, Mrs. Ford and Molly Hines have been recognised but the occasion cannot be recalled.

Lily Symon's Dancing Class

Seen here in preparation for a pre-war carnival are members of the class held in the carnival cave at Turnchapel. Dressed as sailors are Mavis Bond, Irene Burridge, Maureen Roberts, Una Glanville, Gloria Mears, Audrey Morgan, Doris Carpenter, Iris Appelby and one other.

Children at the Wellfield

This photograph is something of a puzzle because none of the children have been recognised and the occasion cannot be recalled. Perhaps it was on the occasion of a local carnival or some form of celebration possibly after the First World War. However, some local children are here and no doubt somebody will eventually remember some of their names.

Carnival Occasion

All assembled for the annual carnival sometime during the 1940s in the football field at Jennycliff. Recognised in the crowd are Dorothy Box, Pauline Demellweek, Theldra Minus, Joyce Allen, Jean Carpenter, Barbara Box and Margaret Carpenter, as part of the crowd with some dressed for the occasion eagerly awaiting the competitions.

Carnival Horse Riding

As part of this popular event an entrant came on horse at the field Jennycliff. Here Mavis Bond is led by Una Glanville watched by friends and spectators some of whom are dressed ready for their part in the event. Charlie Bond is standing on the left of the picture.

The Wellfield in the 1920s

Among this group of men have been recognised Dart Pascho, Barlow Roberts, Reg. Coleman and the boy, Charlie Roberts. The occasion is not known for the group. Military horse training often occurred on the field by troops from Fort Stamford when hurdles and other obstacles were erected for their use during these years. Note the solitary tree in the background which has long gone.

Point Cottages

The many ferrymen who worked from the Point to Oreston lived in these cottages over the years. The ferry was a quick way for getting from Turnchapel to Oreston or to the timber yard where many men worked. One had to hail across the mouth of Hooe Lake and a boat would soon come across for a small charge. One-legged Sam Wright was one of the last to offer this service to local folk.

One Boat and Two Captains

Regular maintenance and cleaning, painting and many other miscellaneous jobs were required by the local fleet of ferries one is here beached next to the pier and being painted in readiness for another season. Many local people were employed by the steamship company, some as captains others as engineers. Captain Harry Tucker is here with pipe in hand who served on the boats; seated is Captain Johns, the piermaster, who was responsible for people entering the boats and clearing them for moving off. He is with his wife by the timbers of the pier.

Local Hurricane in 1962

A victim of a local hurricane which caused considerable havoc and high water. This was the local boat, *Swift*, seen here almost submerged next to the pier. She was later beached and repaired. In the background are the *John W. MacKay* and the *MacKay Bennet*, two cable laying ships which formerly worked out from the depot at Turnchapel.

Hooe Lake Moorings

Three of the fleet of boats worked by the Oreston and Turnchapel Steamboat Company, the *Lively*, *Lady Beatrice* and *City of Plymouth* are moored over winter here in 1930. The company closed in 1957 but once had many boats for ferrying people to and from Plymouth and for pleasure trip work around the local area. Hooe Lake was a convenient nearby spot for mooring boats some of which finished up as living quarters or as hulks for holding goods.

The *Swift* at the Pier

The *Swift* can be seen here moored at the pier from which thousands have crossed the water to Plymouth; at times queues formed right along its length and up the road. The waiting room is here although the original turnstiles have gone. In the background are the *Lively* and the *Dart*, at their normal moorings.

Three Local Men
Seen above are Samuel Rowe, school attendance officer, Grandpa George Hine, landlord of the *Castle Inn*, at Mount Batten, and Robert Barlace, a local boat builder.

An early Boat
This photograph was found among a local collection of material depicting one of the many boats which put out to sea when ships got into difficulties.

The Pier, Turnchapel
This photograph was taken in the 1960s; Mr. Angrove, Alf Tugwell and Claude Mears are standing in front of Jack Oates' house, now gone. He was one of the last permanent ferrymen to work between Turnchapel and Cattedown, the charge for crossing being 2d. He also brought in barrels of beer for the *New Inn* rolling them up the slope seen in the picture and across the road.

The Cattewater
This very early view of the water is believed to date from the turn of the century and was taken from the Point, here seen at low tide. The man has not been recognised but the various masted ships are reminders of the many years they served local needs and made an interesting scene when moored on the water. The house on the right was the foreman's dwelling overlooking the Oreston "pickle yard".

Plaques of Local Interest

These three show aspects of Turnchapel; one for *Lawrence of Arabia*, the other for the now gone Jubilee Hall built for the seamen and the last for the landing point for any ferrymen bringing passengers over from the Plymouth side of the Cattewater.

Aerial View of Turnchapel during the 1930s

This very good aerial view of Turnchapel was taken in the early 1930s probably on a Sunday morning as all the ferry boats are at their moorings and the usual fishing boats are absent from the waterside. There are many interesting features here, a few now gone but others still present. Some of these are (from left to right) six oil tanks and a pumping house which were destroyed during the Second World War, railway station, signal box and track, cable storage area in the former Turnchapel Dockyard, the New Pier, two cable laying ships, the *Marie Louise* and *MacKay Bennett*, the empty slipways, the large Quarry field behind the houses and, at the back, is Hooe and Hooe Lake partly surrounded with open fields. Two craft on the mud flats have been recognised as the schooner, *John Sims*, and a barge named, *Bulla*. Many other smaller features can probably be picked out by the older residents of Turnchapel and Hooe.

Mount Batten Auxiliary Coastguard Drill

Many local men have served in this worthy cause by giving up spare time and turning out at a moment's notice when vessels are in danger of being wrecked or lives at risk along the nearby coastline. Regular training for these eventualities is essential. These two photographs were taken at North Devon when local men took part in competitive mock rescues using all the normal lifesaving equipment. Among those above are Douglas Mutton, Eric Burridge, Harry and Raymond Howe, Albert and Peter Harris, Jack Ford, senior and junior, Frank Powell, Archie Glanville, Alf. Demellweek, Ron Demellweek, leader, Ted Marlowe, Claude Mears, Sam Dungey, Mr. Lawrence and John Gray. Below in the large group are Claude Mears, Tisher Dungey, Mr. Angrove, Jim Demellweek, Jack Ford, Mr. Lawrence, Frank Powell, Peter Lillicrap and Sam Dungey.

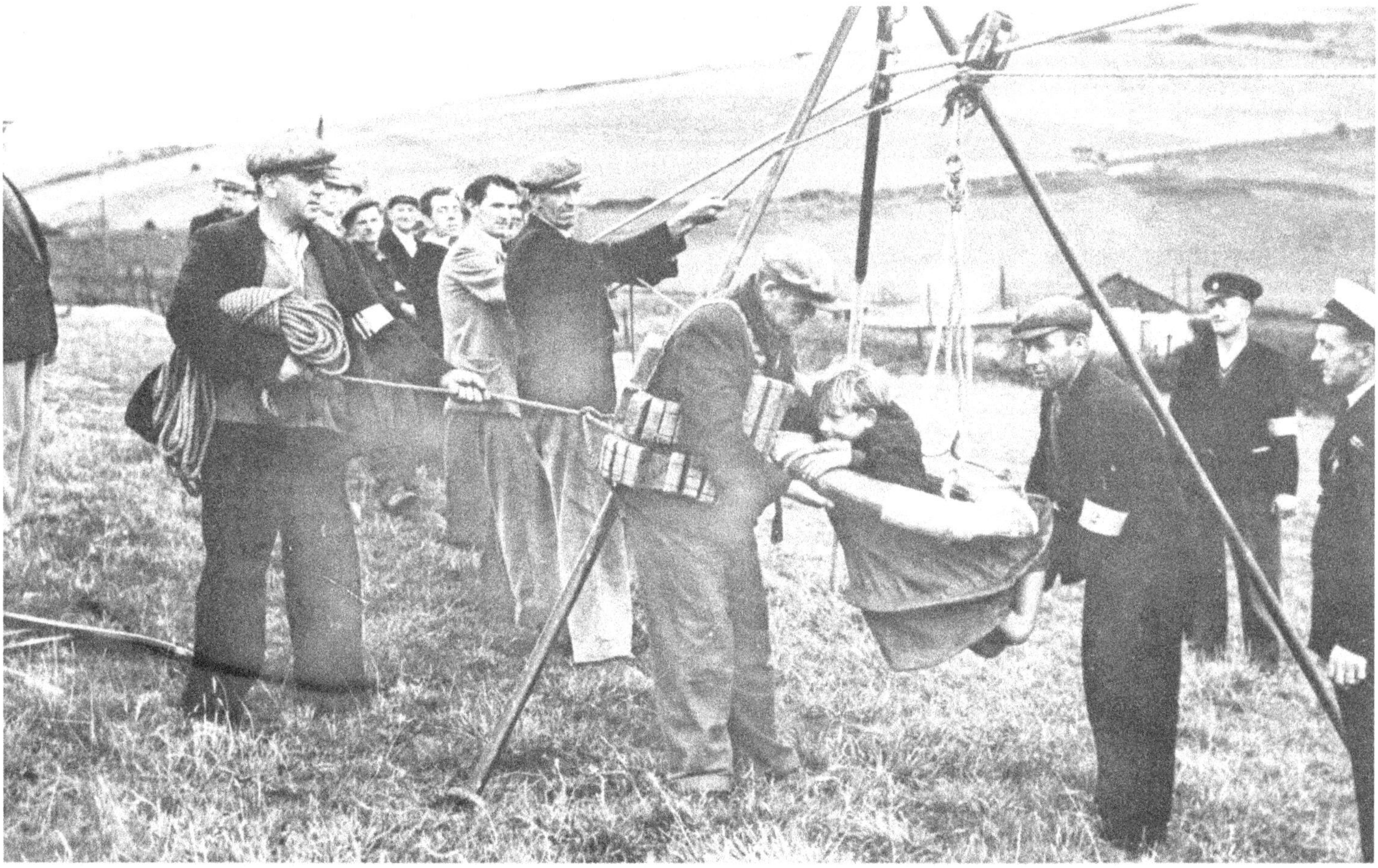

OPENING OF A NEW PIER AT TURNCHAPEL.

A new pier, erected at a cost of £1,000 by Mr. H. Elford, of Oreston, was formally opened yesterday. Owing to the inclement state of the weather there were only a few present from Plymouth. The structure is a substantial work, the piles being of greenheart with iron clamps. It is 1?feet long by 8 feet 6 inches wide, and is protected on the top by strong iron rods. At the end a pretty waiting room has been erected, and benches are provided here and there for the benefit of the passengers. The work was carried out by Messrs. Lapthorne and Gead, of Plymouth, in a very satisfactory manner. The sole right of landing and accommodation belongs to the Oreston and Turnchapel Steamboat Company, whose steamers have plied between the Barbican and Turnchapel for many years. Shortly after two o'clock Mrs. Elford declared the pier open for traffic by unlocking the gate. In a neat little speech she wished the undertaking every success and continued patronage, a sentiment which was greeted with an outburst of cheering. Immediately after, the workmen—numbering about thirty—were entertained to a sumptuous repast by Mr. and Mrs. Elford. There were various attractions on shore, In honour of the event the vicar of the parish (the Rev. J. J. Tapson) provided an excellent tea, at which many of the villagers were entertained. The Oreston and Turnchapel Company has made rapid progress recently, and, within a few days, will add to their present fleet a magnificent steamboat with all the latest improvements. The fife and drum band of the Kitto Institute for working lads were present and contributed a pleasing programme. The inhabitants of the neighbourhood, in appreciation of the gift, liberally subscribed to a fund for the purpose of holding a regatta and sports. A substantial sum was realized, and Mr. B. Rowe officiated as hon. secretary, Messrs. A. Cutts assistant secretary, W. F. Hart treasurer, S. Hinde starter, and Maddick, Willing, Jackson, Ginn and Skelton as committee. There were twelve events on the programme, all, with one exception, being well contested. The men who competed in the different matches were literally supplied with refreshments under the superintendence of Mr. Willing. Great praise is due to the committee for the admirable manner in which they carried out the arrangements in spite of adverse circumstances. The various sports arranged to be held on shore were postponed until next Wednesday afternoon. Following are the events:—

Sailing match for watermen's boats not exceeding 18ft. 5in. Three prizes; six entries—Freada, Froude; Little Dick, Kilton; Souvenir, Oxland; Sophia, Passmore; Watchful, Oats; and Pride of the West, Hugdon.—1, Watchful; 2, Pride of the West; 3, Little Dick.

Four-oared merchant ships' boats. Three prizes; four entries.—1, Eleanor, Harper; 2, Concord, Jackson; 3, Halloween, Northmore.

Two-oared merchant ships' boats. Three prizes; four entries.—1, Elizabeth, Jackson; 2, Halloween; 3, Eleanor, Harper.

Opening of the Pier

This article appeared in a local paper on the occasion of the opening of Turnchapel pier in 1889. It now makes very interesting reading and shows how the occasion was celebrated for it has since proved to have been a great asset for the area although its use has now gone.

Turnchapel at the beginning of the Century

The general view of Turnchapel and part of the Cattewater is thought to date from the opening years of this century. It is the earliest view of the locality in this booklet and will almost certainly bring back many memories of what the waterfront area must have looked like before the changes of more recent years. The pier with its original supporting timbers forms the centrepiece to which a steamer is moving. Various boats are moored up the Cattewater. Grainger's quay is in the foreground then Westlake's coalyard. The living quarters for the men working in the yard and the sheds, together with open areas for chains, forms part of the background to this very interesting picture of the village.

Bird's eye View of Hooe and Turnchapel

These two aerial views of the area clearly show the main features of both localities. The former naval estate dubbed the "Hooe Loos" form a triangle between two roads while the lower picture shows how Turnchapel developed along a fairly narrow strip of land between beach and high cliff and open field. "Sycamore" beach is in the bottom left corner.

Around Hooe Lake

Many photographs could have been included in this book showing things associated with the lake. Here Radford "castle" forms the centre of the dam which holds back part of the higher area of the lake and the chimney and building below still stand as reminders of the once active Hexton Hill Quarry from which stone was shipped out from its small quay.

Boringdon Football Team

The year of this team has not been found but some of its members have been recognised. They are Peter Lillicrap, Bert Wells, Gerald Parnell, Ernest Wells, George Levy, Harry Morgan, W. Tucker, J. Gray and S. Mahon.

Turnchapel and Hooe Athletic Club, 1923/24

This team were the winners in the Devon Association League, Division 1, comprising A. Salmon, E. Vosper, W. Burgoyne, T. Charlick, C. Burgoyne, W. Perry, E. Rogers, A. Dungey, *captain*, J. Cudlip, F. Glanville, J. Hooper, A. Maddick, S. Hall, M. Lorraine, C. Mears, R. Dolton, P. Pascho, G. Charlick, R. Colman and M. Pascho, *chairman*. They are proudly posing with the three cups and the ball used in the game.

Hooe School Football Team, 1933

Proudly displaying their shield and holding the ball this group is made up of Maynard Attwood, Harry Brown, Bob Skilton, Donald Brown, Harry Morgan, H. Vokes, Gordon Whitefield, Jim Cawley, Clifford Oxland, Arthur Pearse and Bert Wells.

School children of Hooe and Turnchapel, 1922

These two photographs were taken at the higher school, Hooe, yet included younger children from the lower school at Turnchapel. The smaller must have walked up from Turnchapel for this photograph which was almost certainly taken on the same day as the upper one. Mr. Edwin Rogers, the headmaster, is seen here with children some identified as Frank Furze, Joe Studwick, Ivy Tucker, Ted Sallows, Frank Rowse, Marg. Oates, George Duncan, Tom Jackman, Lloyd Body, Bill Salmon, Jack Gale, Bob Skilton, Wilf England, Ivy Vokes, Hilma Glinn, Fred Tucker and Les. Macinearn. Mrs. Redstone, Mrs. Vincent and Mrs. Heslick are the teachers with the children in the lower group some recognised as Bob Duncan, Alec Slocombe, Victor Cockerel, George and Arthur Glinn, Amy and Audrey Dale, Dorothy Couling, Hedley Doddridge, Albert Thomas, Edward Gill, Paul Rogers, Arthur Oxland, Harry Brown, Ivy Lillicrap, Leonard Smale, William Oates, Edith Wells, Edith Roberts, Ernie Appleby and George Siggers. Miss Nott, headmistress, is sat next to Mr. Rogers.

Three Views of Hooe Lane

These postcard views show the main road approach to Hooe and Turnchapel sometime before the last war (1939-45) conveniently including one or two people and vehicles. Times have certainly changed! The upper shot shows Harwood's bread van coming down the hill past the *Victoria Inn* and a parked Austin car. The cyclist is Mr. Henry Hurrell off to work at Friary Station during the 1920s.

Mr. William Richards is walking back from Plymouth probably returning with goods for his confectionery shop or ice bought in the Barbican for keeping ice cream cold. His donkey, *Mary*, was well known in the village making this weekly journey with punctual regularity. There were no delivery vans then!

The photograph below shows Mr. F. Harris, farmer, talking to Mr. Shillabeer, the roadman in 1920. He was responsible for the upkeep of the local roads and trimming the hedges. The part cut was where the village pump used to be while opposite the cottages with the shelter-like porches are still there. Then one was a sweet shop, ran by Mrs. B. Richards, another was a bakery and Mr. Philip Hine, farmer, lived in the large house where the car is parked. Mr. and Mrs. T. Pearse lived in the cottage above the former sweet shop.

Commemorative Tree

This plaque records the ceremony performed by Lady Roborough of opening the infants' school in 1956. Hooe Junior school was opened in 1931 taking over the role of educating local children from the St. John's Church school which was next to the church. Both schools serve the area and have grown to meet the needs of new families coming here to live.

Some Men of the Locality

Arthur Glinn is seen here somewhere in the area taking a rest from a long cycle ride. A keen cyclist he often covered many miles in one day on what looks a heavy machine with no gears! Cycling was once very popular and frequently the only means of getting around the area in spite of rough roads. This photograph dates before the First World War. A fine group of local men pose for the photographer outside the *Royal Oak Inn* prior to what must be an outing of some kind. The buttonholes and dress, with the bowler hats, suggests that they are expected to look their best for the occasion. Recognised among them are Nat. Pine, landlord of the *Royal Oak*, Samuel Phillips, Arthur Glinn, Lawyer Hawkins, Jack Edwards, Walter Lillicrap, Harry Smith, George Lillicrap, with others round the year 1917.

A pre-war Carnival

All dressed for another of the very popular pre-war carnivals some local people and visitors are seen here on the Wellfield, Turnchapel, ready to enter the fancy dress competition. Mr. Morgan, Puddy Phillpots of the *No Place Inn*, Plymouth, Bessie Dungey, as the Queen, and Mr. W. M. Perry are recognised in the group together with Hilda Pearse.

Turnchapel Juniors A.F.C. 1921/22

Seen here on their home pitch at Higher Hooe are M. Pyne, landlord of the *Royal Oak*, J. Atkins, Mr. Paget, B. Charlick, Dart Pascho, Dick Richards, in uniform, R. Dolton, Harry Burridge, Nippey Dungey, Messrs. Glanville, Roberts, Demellweek, Elliot and Cowling ready for another vigorous game of local football.

Char-a-banc to Princetown

All set for a day's outing from where the school gates are now sited. Mrs. A. Slocombe organised this trip for local people which include Alice Pearse, Thomas Pearse. Gran. Hurrell, Eileen Wright, Alice Doney, George Pearse and others sometime during 1922. The open-topped coach came out from Plymouth; note the hard tyres and large headlamps!

Hexton Hill

Two early views of this part of Hooe are shown on this page the first (1938) looking up the hill towards the old cottages which formerly crowded this narrow road going to Hexton Quay and Quarry. New houses were built in 1977. A few remains of this local enterprise can still be seen including the prominent chimney and sheds close to Hooe Lake. Hexton House has an interesting past. It was converted into a bakery during the 1880s to supply bread to the troops stationed in Fort Stamford and Fort Staddon. This lasted until 1903 when the army undertook its own baking. The house was then put to use as a butchers shop by the new owner, Mr. E. Wakeham of Oreston. This business flourished until 1932 when the building reverted to a private house.

Mr Ernest Berry with son and daughter, Ernest and Iris, together James and Maude Drake with Wifrid Drake are seen in the other picture (1928) part way down Yonder Street. This view will probably surprise many newcomers to the area as it shows the old narrow street with washing drying between the houses! A lot of new building work has taken place here on sites formerly occupied by very small dwellings which today would be considered inadequate for normal living standards.

High water on Hooe Lake gives Ernest Berry an opportunity to prepare his clinker-built boat for a sail probably out down the Cattewater to do a spot of fishing in the Sound.

The Railway to Turnchapel

These five pictures show some aspects of this once popular line the train being dubbed the "Turnchapel Flyer". The service started on 4th October, 1896, from Friary Station, and the last train left Turnchapel on 8th September, 1951. It had a chequered career during the last war when it was used by troops and damaged in air raids. It was originally part of the London and South Western Railway. The top picture shows a 0.4.4 side tank engine passing Lucas Terrace Halt in 1935 on its way to Turnchapel, the manually operated swing over the entrance to Hooe Lake is seen under maintenance work while Mark Bow is crossing it in the upper picture. Jack Lambert was also a signalman on his line. The small station on the loop is below and the rebuilt signal box. The great oil tank blaze at Turnchapel in the war caused damage to the track and to the original signal box.

TURNCHAPEL.

Clergy and Gentry.

Hughes Mr. George
Hughes John, commander R.N.
Tapson Rev. James John, M.A., The Vicarage
Usborne Alexander Borne, Esq., captain R.N., Whitestock villa

Trades and Professions.

Aggaford John, shoemaker
Bennett John, builder and contractor
BENNETT JOHN HENRY, stone and marble mason, painter, plumber, and glazier, and assistant overseer, Amberly cottages
BURLACE ALFRED, yacht and boat-builder
Brown John, waterman
Chapman William, waterman
Collis William, pilot
Cullis William, limestone and coaldealer
Darton Isaac, boatbuilder
Dean Abraham, shoemaker
Dean Henry Richard, shoemaker
Doddridge William, " New Inn "
Edwards Mrs. Jane, baker
Frood John, " Shipwrights' Arms "
Glinn Edward, pilot
Glinn John H., pilot
Glinn Richard, pilot
Glinn William, pilot
Hart William, coal and limedealer
Hine George, " Castle " inn, Mount Batten
Irving William, waterman
Kelly Mrs. Caroline, shopkeeper
Kelly William, baker and grocer
Moore and Babb, ochre and brick manufacturers
Oats James, master mariner
Pascoe William, waterman
Pinck Mrs. Susan, shopkeeper
Ridway Charles, harbour pilot
Ryder Abraham, " Boringdon Arms "
Tringore John, waterman and shopkeeper
Walke Richard, ship and house carpenter
Wyatt John, waterman

Post Office—Wall Letter Box cleared at 3.45 p.m. Sundays 8.15 a.m.

National School—William Bamkin, master; Mrs. Bamkin, mistress
Infant School—Mrs. Williams, mistress

Hooe, 1¾ miles west-by-south, was formed into an ecclesiastical parish May 9, 1856. St. John's church, erected in 1855, is a building of stone in the Early English style, consisting of chancel, nave, aisles, south porch and a turret containing 2 bells. The register dates from the year 1855. The living is a vicarage, gross yearly value £400 (£75 of which is paid by the War Office and Admiralty), net £319, with residence, in the gift of Keble College, Oxford, and held since 1870 by the Rev. James John Tapson, of Corpus Christi college, Cambridge. The principal landowners are the War Office and John Bayly esq. The area is 770 acres; the population in 1891 was 1,364.

MOUNT BATTEN, BOVISAND, STADDISCOMBE, STAMFORD, WEST HOOE and TURNCHAPEL are in this parish.

WALL LETTER BOXES.—West Hooe, cleared at 8.15 & 10.15 a.m. & 6.10 p.m.; sundays at 10.15 a.m.; & Pomphlett, cleared at 10.55 a.m. & 7 p.m. week days only

SCHOOLS :—
National (mixed), erected in 1855, for 124 children; average attendance, 95; Francis Wyatt, master
National (infants), Turnchapel; average attendance, 59; Mrs. Jago, mistress
Railway Station (L. & S. W. R.), Thomas Furze

Hooe is another hamlet, about 1¼ mile from Plymstock; and Bovisand, a continuation of this hamlet, contains extensive fortifications, which have just been erected by Government, also a Coast Guard Station. The vessels of the navy are here supplied with water from a reservoir about half-a-mile inland, from whence it is brought in pipes. In 1856 this was created a separate ecclesiastical district, and a small church, dedicated to St. John, was erected. The living is a vicarage, valued at £79 per annum, in the incumbency of the Rev. James John Tapson, M.A., and the patronage of Lady Rogers.

TURNCHAPEL is another hamlet of this parish, also on the banks of the Catwater, in which are extensive fortifications, called Fort Stamford, which have recently been erected by Government on Staddon heights. The rifle butts of the Plymouth Volunteers are situated at Mount Batten. The ancient round tower, which was originally erected by the Parliamentarians during their occupation of Plymouth, is now used as a signal station.

HOOE.

Clergy and Gentry.

Bulteel Francis Feeke, Esq., Thorn cottage
Hare Major William Henry, Retreat
Hart Mr. John, Fanshaw cottage
Hicks Colonel Thomas William, Bellevue
Moggridge Lieut.-Colonel John Yerbury, R.E.
Tapson Rev. James John, M.A., vicar, West Hooe

Trades and Professions.

Beard John, gardener, Higher Hooe
Bennett William, " Royal Oak "
Creed Daniel, shopkeeper
Hart Mrs. Sarah and William, limestone merchants
Hine Philip, farmer, West Hooe Barton
Hughes Mr. George
Maddock James, baker
Repath Charles, carpenter
Repath Robert, farmer
Redpath Robert, tea and fruit gardens, West Hooe
Stephens Andrew, " Victoria " inn

Trade directories usually contain lists of people, businesses and commercial information which have been produced every few years since the 1850s. These extracts for Hooe and Turnchapel now make interesting reading as they recall, quite accurately, probably all the commercial activities for the years shown.

HOOE.

Belcher John Waring, Whitestock
Bulteel Percy Henry, Higher Hooe
Bulteel Mrs. Thorn cottage, West Hooe
Hicks Miss, Bellevue house
Hurrell James, Hexton cottage
Longfield William Digby (Fleet-Surgeon R.N.), St. Ann's
Popplestone The Misses, Hooe
Popplestone Samuel, Hooe

COMMERCIAL.

Ball Alfred Ernest, watch maker
Burgoyne John, carpenter, Lower Hooe
Burgoyne Samuel, baker, Lower Hooe
Cole Annie Maria (Mrs.), btchr. Low. Hooe
Darton Isaac Brace, boat builder, Mount Batten
Drake Eli, carpenter, Turnchapel
Ford William Hy. Victoria inn, Hooe
Gould Edward Henry, farmer, Manor farm, Staddiscombe
Harris Thos. tea & fruit grdns. Low. Hooe
Hewings Irenia (Mrs.), Royal Oak P.H
Hine Geo. The Castle P.H. Mount Batten
Hine Philip, farmer, Staddiscombe
Hine Phillip Bluett, farmer, West Hooe
Kelly Wm. Sl. ship builder, Mount Batten
Maddick Anthony, baker, West Hooe
Oborne Henry, grocer, West Hooe
Pearse Ths. frmr. Leyford, Staddiscombe
Peathyjohns Jn. tea grdns. Higher Hooe
Rapson Robert, shopkeeper & market gardener, Staddiscombe
Wakeham Ernest, butcher, West Hooe
Widdicombe Frederick William, Shipwrights' Arms P.H

1893

Hooe.

PRIVATE RESIDENTS.

Brinsley Daniel Henry, Whitestock
Bulteel Mrs. Thorn cottage, West Hooe
Chapell William, West Hooe
Cullis William, Wellfield vils. Turnchapel
Glinn Mrs. Turnchapel
Hare Miss, Higher Hooe
Hardy Philip, Mansion ho. Turnchapel
Hicks Col. Thomas Wm. Bellevue house
Longfield William Digby, St. Ann's
Mills Edward, Turnchapel
Mills Mrs. Turnchapel
Oats William King, Turnchapel
Popplestone The Misses, Hooe
Popplestone Samuel, Hooe
Tapson Rev. James John M.A. [vicar], Turnchapel
Williams Mrs. Hexton cottage

COMMERCIAL.

Blight Mary (Mrs.), shpkpr. Turnchapel
Brown Charles, New inn, Turnchapel
Burlace Alfred, boat builder, Turnchapel
Burgoyne John, carpenter, Lower Hooe
Burgoyne Samuel, baker, Lower Hooe
Cole AnnMaria (Mrs.), butchr. Low. Hooe
Coleman George, grocer, Turnchapel
Cullis William, quarry owner, Turnch'pl
Darton Isaac, boat builder, Mount Batten
Dean Hy. Richd. shoe maker, Turnchapel
Drake Joseph, carpenter, Turnchapel
Ford William Hy. Victoria inn, Hooe
George James, Royal Oak P.H
Gould Edward Henry, farmer, Manor farm, Staddiscombe
Gurney George R.A. sergeant instructor, Turnchapel
Harris Thos. tea & fruit grdns. Low. Hooe
Hart Wm. limestone quarry, Turnchapel
Hine Geo. The Castle P.H. Mount Batten
Hine Philip, farmer, Staddiscombe
Hine Phillip John, farmer, West Hooe
Hobbs John, Shipwrights' Arms P.H
Kelly Elizth. (Mrs.), baker, Turnchapel
Maddick Anthony, baker, West Hooe
Oborne Henry, grocer, West Hooe
Pearse Thos. frmr. Leeford, Staddiscombe
Peathyjohns Wm. tea grdns. Higher Hooe
Rapson Robt. shopkeeper, Staddiscombe
Rowe Samuel, boot maker, Turnchapel
Skilton Henry, pilot, Turnchapel
Walke Richard, carpenter, Turnchapel
Westlake James, coal mrchnt. Turnchapl
Williams John Henry, Borringdon Arms P.H. Turnchapel
Willing Samuel, grocer, Post office, Turnchapel

Turnchapel.

Cullis William, Wellfield villas
Fox George Crocker
Mills Edward
Oaks William King
Skilton Henry
Tapson Rev. James John M.A. [vicar]

COMMERCIAL.

Blight Mary (Mrs.), shopkeeper
Brown Charles, New inn
Burlace Alfred, boat builder
Coleman George, grocer
Dean William Henry, shoe maker
Drake Eli, carpenter
Fellows Charles Grincell, sergeant instructor R.A
Hart William, Limestone quarry
Kelly John Dean, baker
Rogers William, Borringdon Arms P.H
Rowe William, boot maker
Westlake James, coal merchant
Willing Samuel, grocer, Post office

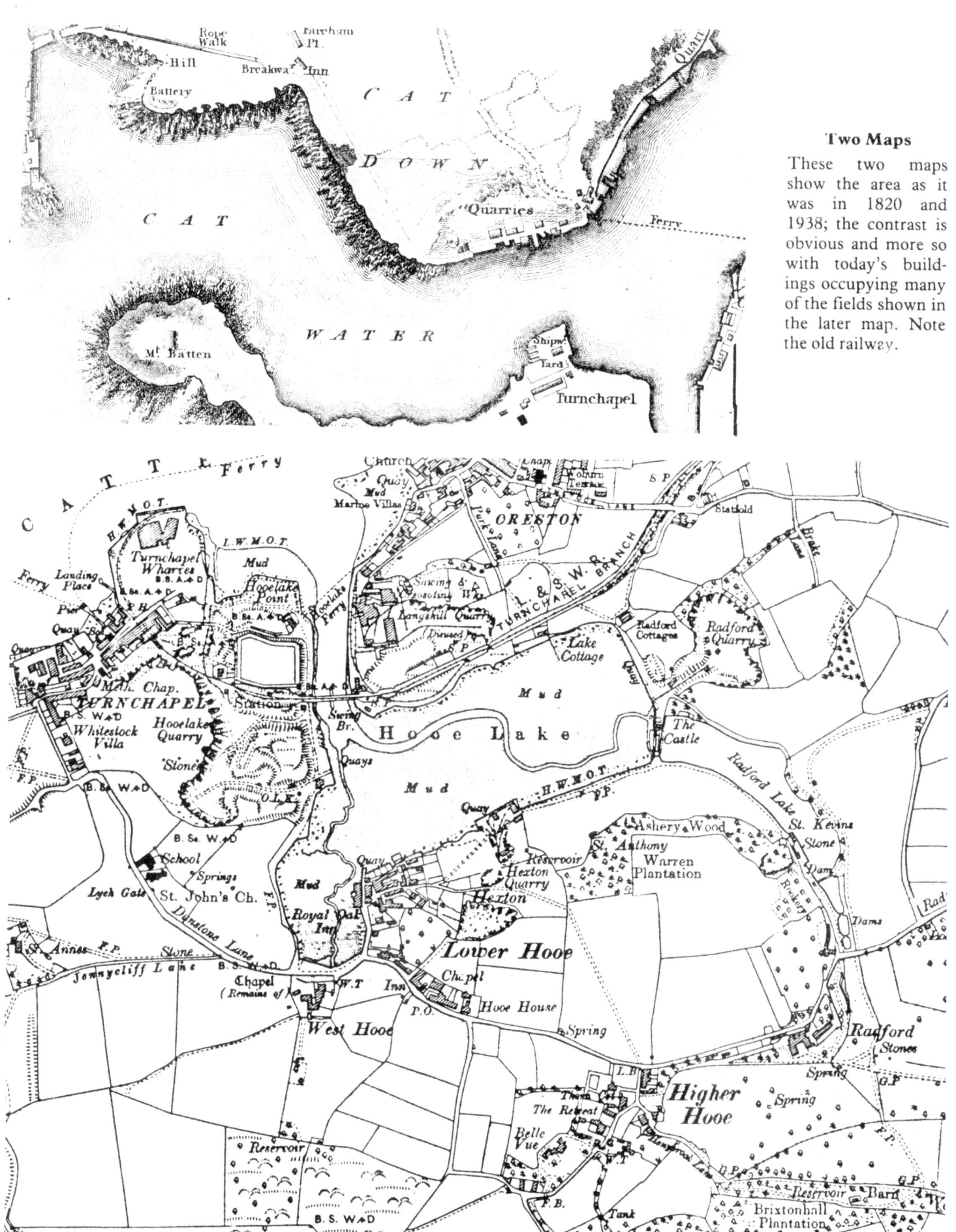

Two Maps

These two maps show the area as it was in 1820 and 1938; the contrast is obvious and more so with today's buildings occupying many of the fields shown in the later map. Note the old railway.

Pilot Boats

These were used for guiding or piloting in large sailing vessels into the Sound and then to a mooring either up the Cattewater or elsewhere. A good knowledge of local tides, rocks, etc., was essential and for this work two local families vied with each in getting business by racing well out in the Channel and trying to put aboard a pilot first. The Glinns and the Skiltons undertook this and used three boats one of which is here. One to three was for Turnchapel craft and higher numbers came from Cawsand.

Mount Batten from Turnchapel

This early nineteenth century engraving shows the Cattewater partly crowded with various craft against the background of the Barbican and the Royal Citadel upon the Hoe. Mount Batten tower stands prominent on the headland below which are a few houses, the beach and foreground of the Turnchapel area. Access from the village to Mount Batten and its *Castle Inn* was direct and easy in those days.

A Local "Flash" Boat

This boat was specially built for racing, hence the name, and shows W. Salmon, Tister Holden, Arthur Glinn, George Allen and Nippy Dungey as crew. The boat was called *Scotty* and came from Mr. Woodley of the *Shipwrights Arms*. The rear boat was *The Hustler*. Note the old turnstiles on the pier which were there in the 1930s. Flash boats featured prominently in all local regattas around the Plymouth area.

Arthur L. Clamp – the man behind the books

Arthur Leslie Clamp was a man of boundless energy with a passion for helping others, particularly through his love of history. A printer by trade, he started his career in a printing company before moving his family from Exeter to Plymouth to teach at the Plymouth College of Art and Design, where he eventually became the Head of the Printing Department.

Arthur with his five children.

A Devoted Family Man

Despite his love of teaching, Arthur prioritised his family, always making it home by 5:30pm for tea. He and his wife, Rosemary, raised five children: Susan, Angela, Elizabeth, David, and Steven. Arthur would often combine his love of family and history by taking his children on Sunday walks, encouraging them to appreciate historical monuments by taking photos or making crayon rubbings of gravestones for his books. The family home at 203 Elburton Road was a hub of activity, with a large garden, featuring a two-storey fort and a makeshift swimming pool.

A Lifelong Learner and Adventurer

Arthur's thirst for knowledge extended beyond history to a deep curiosity about the world. He was passionate about exploring different cultures, traditions, and cuisines, often taking advantage of his long summer holidays as a teacher to travel to places like India, Russia, South America, the middle east and the USA, sometimes bringing one of his children along. This adventurous spirit even influenced his home life, as seen by the short-lived family tradition of steam-cooking vegetables after a trip to Iceland.

History is a prominent feature of family days out

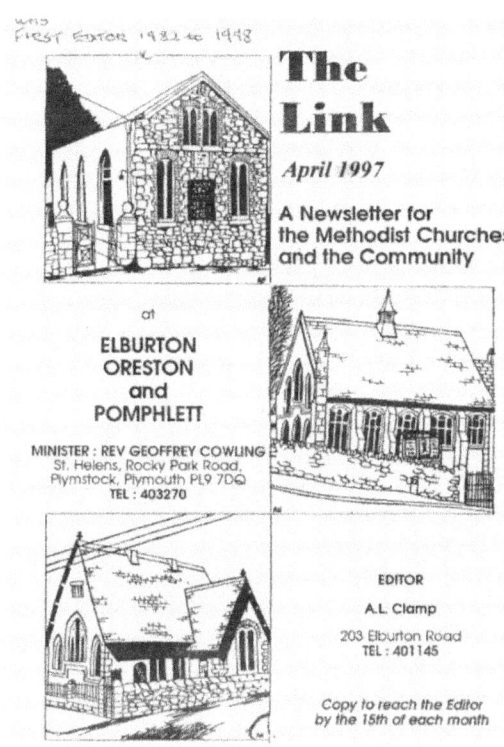

Community and Philanthropic Spirit

His commitment to serving others was evident in his long-standing involvement with the Elburton Methodist Church. He was the Sunday School Superintendent for over 15 years and served as the editor of the wider church's monthly newsletter, "The Link," for a similar duration. After Rosemary's very sad passing, Arthur later remarried and, following a chance encounter with a professor from India, established a connection with a missionary school in Chennai. Together with his new wife, Christine, he co-founded a "Sponsor a Child's Education" program that continues to this day.

Pictured left – The cover of 'The Link' complete with hand drawn sketches of each church by Angela
Below right – Arthur Clamp promoting his latest book
Below left – Arthur at home with his first wife, Rosemary
Below centre – Arthur on holiday with his second wife, Christine

A Legacy of Learning and Positivity

Arthur's greatest passion was history, which he brought to life through tireless research, documentation, and the many books he authored. He was driven by a need to "never be stuck in a rut," constantly seeking new experiences, meeting new people, and expanding his knowledge. With a positive attitude and a great sense of humour, he was always ready to help others, leaving a lasting impact on his family and community. His children, Susan, Angela, Elizabeth, David, and Steven, remember him with love and gratitude.

David Clamp, 2025

A Legacy of Local History

Below is the story of how Arthur L Clamp began writing books, in his own words, drafted shortly before he passed away in 2001. I have only made minor alterations to this text, correcting grammatical errors that he did not survive to correct himself. When I first discovered this text, I was shocked to see my name mentioned. It seems that, unbeknownst to me, I shared my first PC with him. I suspect he used it during the day when I was at school, although I do have one memory of sitting with him and showing him how it worked. It has been a pleasure to pick up where he left off and see his books republished and redistributed, and to know that I was part of the story, even back then. It was also fascinating to discover that his pricing structure matches the way I have tried to price the books, with a third going to local sellers and the rest covering printing costs with a little left over for my expenses.

I am his eldest grandson, and it is a privilege to curate his legacy, which we are calling 'The Clamp Collection'. The very last line of the text originally reads "The following pages list all the titles." Sadly, that page is missing and we have no record of all the books he published and knowing that some of those were researched by other authors makes the process of finding them even harder. I look forward to one day completing the collection and seeing them all available again. And maybe, one day, I'll even start writing my own to add to the series. For now, here is his story in his own words.

Steven Gibson, 2025

Writing and Publishing Booklets on Local Topics and Areas

I started this interest in either 1968 or 1969 when living in Woodford. I had by these dates established the Department of Printing and I think I must have been looking for something different to do. The first titles were of A5 size proofed from type set at Clarke, Doble and Brendon, Ltd., Plymouth printers, and then made up into pages and printed at Sawtell and Neilson, Ltd., Totnes.

Then began a slow process of getting them out to shops, etc. which proved to be more time consuming and difficult than actually researching, writing and getting the books into print. However, I persisted and opened a business account with Barclays Bank on the Broadway. I was advised to give it a title so I called it "Westway Publications". There came along another problem, one of storage of paper and finished books which was solved when the family moved to Elburton in 1970.

I changed the printer to Penwell, Ltd., Callington, Cornwall, as he was then just setting up himself and his prices seemed very reasonable. I did not get any of the printers to make up the complete books. I hand folded the flat printed sheets, stitched the books on a small manual table stitcher and trimmed them in a small hand turned guillotine which I bought from someone in Penzance for £40. It was brought up in a van.

The trouble and time going to and fro to Callington was too much so I transferred the printing to PDS Printers, Prince Rock, Plymouth, and I have been with them ever since. Now they are at Plympton which is easy to reach and they fold the flat sheets which was turning out to be a long chore which only saved a small part of the printing costs.

All my first titles were written by myself. I took the photographs and developed them in the loft of the house, the type was set by now on a computer situated in the house at Elburton from which I had collected photographic lengths of text to cut up and law down as pages.

At some point I decided that I would do my own film processing of lith film so I bought a large second hand process camera from Kingsbridge and learnt through trial and error to make line negatives of the text and halftone negatives of the illustrations which proved more difficult than I anticipated. The main problem was trying to keep the developer in the large dish at the correct temperature as any change would affect the developing time. I replaced this old camera with a brand new one bought from Croydon, Surrey, costing £900. This has turned out to be a great asset cutting out an expensive part of the printer's costs and one crucial aspect of the work which I could control.

By the middle 1970s there were many outlets I had contacted in Plymouth, up to Dartmoor, Exeter, around to Torbay, Totnes, Dartmouth and the South Hams. The market for local books was much greater than I had first thought and through getting to know many local people undertaking research themselves had the chance to help and make up books for other people who had in most instances, got together a collection of photographs with some text in a rather muddled way. Through my experience in print I was able to shape up their work and get it into print and in every case I had to pay the printer and let the person have the royalties. In the majority of titles produced in this manner this was another way of producing titles and it did give some profit to my work. However, I must say that in a few cases I lost out by either the other person getting the numbers wrong, not returning any monies from stock I delivered or they thought that more of their books should have been sold.

The print run was usually 1,000 copies and from time to time I have had reprints of 250 copies. It took about ten years to clear the first print run so I always had large stocks in the garage, workshop, etc. The numbers sold during the early years was about 7,000 copies a year increasing to around 9,000 copies and for the whole of the enterprise about 500,000 have been sold. The booklets have become part of the local scene and many people collect them, shops regularly order copies and I go around certain areas month by month restocking or replacing titles as necessary.

During the past year or so I have started setting the text on a Packard Bell PC, something which I should have done some years back. I share it with Steven Gibson, my grandson. There appears to be no end to the market for local books, but I could not earn a regular income because of the long time it takes to sell stock.

However, now exceeding 100 titles made up mainly of A4 twenty-four page booklets, some folded guides, with selling prices set with a third going to the shop which is the trade custom, the original idea has been quite successful and could go on for ever.

Apart from monetary benefits, however spasmodically these might be, I have learnt a lot myself, met many interesting people and have become part of the local scene with requests to give talks and to advise people about getting into print.

Arthur L Clamp, 2001

This newspaper article, published by the Evening Herald on 17th August 2001, forms a good record of his life. Just as he encourages us to learn more about local history, we encourage you to learn a little about him. For that reason, we have included these pages at the back of all the most recently republished books, in honour of his memory and recognition of his contribution to the community.

www.ingramcontent.com/pod-product-compliance
Lightning Source LLC
Chambersburg PA
CBHW061404070526
44584CB00031B/4157